CUPCAKE BAKERY

The Most Delicious, Easy-to-make Cupcake Recipes Ever

(The Ultimate Cupcake Recipes in One Place)

Kevin Milligan

Published by Sharon Lohan

© **Kevin Milligan**

All Rights Reserved

Cupcake Bakery: The Most Delicious, Easy-to-make Cupcake Recipes Ever (The Ultimate Cupcake Recipes in One Place)

ISBN 978-1-7776245-5-2

All rights reserved. No part of this guide may be reproduced in any form without permission in writing from the publisher except in the case of brief quotations embodied in critical articles or reviews.

Legal & Disclaimer

The information contained in this book is not designed to replace or take the place of any form of medicine or professional medical advice. The information in this book has been provided for educational and entertainment purposes only.

The information contained in this book has been compiled from sources deemed reliable, and it is accurate to the best of the Author's knowledge; however, the Author cannot guarantee its accuracy and validity and cannot be held liable for any errors or omissions. Changes are periodically made to this book. You must consult your doctor or get professional medical advice before using any of the suggested remedies, techniques, or information in this book.

Table of contents

Part 1 1

Introduction 2

1. Vanilla Cupcakes With Swiss Meringue Buttercream Frosting 3
2. Red Velvet Cupcakes With Cream Cheese Frosting 5
3. Cookies And Cream Cupcakes With Cream Frosting 8
4. Sticky Toffee Cupcakes With Caramel Buttercream Frosting 10
5. Carrot Cake And Cream Cheese Frosting 13
6. Raspberry Cupcakes With Swiss Meringue Buttercream Frosting 15
7. Mocha Cupcakes With Cream Frosting 18
8. Lemon Cupcakes With Lemon Flavored Cream Cheese Frosting 20
9. Chocolate Cupcakes With Ganache Frosting 22
10. Tiramisu Cupcakes 25
11. Coconut Cupcakes With Cream Cheese Frosting 28
12. Matcha Cupcakes With Cream Frosting 30
13. Pumpkin Cupcakes With Cream Cheese Frosting 32
14. Black Forest Cupcakes With Cream Frosting 34
15. Chocolate Chip Cookie Dough Cupcakes With Ganache Frosting 37

16. Dulce De Leche Cupcakes With Dulce De Leche Buttercream Frosting..40

17. Birthday Cake Cupcakes With Buttercream Sprinkled Frosting..42

18. Gingerbread Cupcakes With Caramel Cream Cheese Frosting..44

19. Apple Pie Cupcakes With Cream Frosting..............................47

20. Nutella Cupcakes With Nutella Frosting.................................49

21. Peanut Butter Cupcakes With Ganache Frosting.................52

22. Rafaello Cupcakes With Rafaello Cream Cheese Frosting 54

23. Lotus Biscoff Cupcakes With Cream Frosting......................58

24. Banana Cupcakes With Brown Butter Cream Cheese Frosting..60

25. Hummingbird Cupcakes With Cream Cheese Frosting.....63

26. Strawberry Cheesecake Cupcakes With Cream Cheese Frosting..65

27. Peaches And Cream Cupcakes..68

28. Salted Caramel Cupcakes With Caramel Buttercream Frosting..70

29. Blueberry Cupcakes With White Chocolate Blueberry Buttercream Frosting..73

30. Orange Cupcakes With Cream Frosting.................................75

Conclusion..78

Part 2..79

Introduction	80
Cupcakes Recipes	81
Double Vanilla Cupcakes	81
Vanilla & Cranberry Cream Cupcakes	83
Vanilla & Blueberry Cupcakes	84
Chocolate & Butter Cream Cupcakes	86
Brown Sugar Cupcakes	88
Blackberry & Raspberry Cream Cupcakes	89
Butter Cream Roses	91
Chocolate & Cream Cheese Cupcakes	93
Hazelnuts & Caramel Cupcakes	94
Chocolate & Coconut Cupcakes	96
Black Forest Cupcakes	98
Chocolate & Cream & Raspberries Cupcakes	100
Vanilla & Cream & Strawberry Cupcakes	101
Vanilla & Blackberry Cream Cupcakes	104
Chocolate & Cinnamon Anise Cream Cupcakes	105
Vanilla And Strawberry Cream Cupcakes	107
Chocolate & Caramel Cream Cupcakes	108
Pumpkin Cream Cupcakes	110
Raspberry Jam & Cream Cupcakes	112
Vanilla & Banana Cream	114
Oreo Cupcakes	115

Vanilla & Peach Cream Cupcakes 117

Pumpkin Spice & Cream Cupcakes 119

Vanilla & Blackberry Cream Cupcakes 120

Part 1

Introduction

Whether you're gearing up for a bake sale or simply want to treat yourself or your loved ones (cupcakes as gifts anybody?) to something sweet, you need to look no further than this recipe book. You'll find 30 of the most mouth-watering cupcake recipes here, along with frosting recipes for each cupcake flavor.

Ranging from traditional flavors like vanilla and chocolate to more trendy flavors like matcha and cookie butter, this recipe book has it all. And the best part about these cupcakes are that most of them come together in less than hour! Each recipe in this book yields a dozen cupcakes but they can easily be halved, doubled or tripled, depending on the occasion. Detailed, step-by-step instructions are provided along with suggestions for toppings that will guarantee the most delicious batch of cupcakes you have ever eaten. So what are you waiting for? Choose a recipe (or 2 or 3) and get baking!

1. Vanilla Cupcakes With Swiss Meringue Buttercream Frosting

Moist and fluffy vanilla cupcakes with the best buttercream frosting ever.

Makes: 12 cupcakes

Prep: 25 mins

Bake: 15 mins

Ingredients:

For the cupcakes:

- 1 ¼ cups all-purpose flour
- 1 cup white sugar
- 1 ½ baking powder
- ½ tsp salt
- ½ cup milk
- ¼ cup vegetable oil
- ½ tbsp. vanilla extract
- 1 large egg

- ½ cup water

For the frosting:

- 2 egg whites
- ¾ cup white sugar
- ¾ cup unsalted butter, softened and cut into squares
- 1 tsp vanilla extract
- Pinch of salt
- Sprinkles, for decoration

Directions:

For the cupcakes:

Preheat oven to 350°F and line a cupcake pan with 12 liners.

In a large bowl, whisk together the dry ingredients and set aside.

In a medium bowl, combine the milk, oil and vanilla. Add in the egg and whisk until well combined.

Slowly add in the milk and egg mixture to the dry ingredients and whisk until well combined.

Add in the water and whisk until smooth. Do not overmix.

Pour batter into cupcake liners, filling the liners half way up.

Bake for about 15 minutes or until a toothpick put into the centre of a cupcake comes out with a few crumbs.

Cool cupcakes on a cooling rack.

For the frosting:

In the bowl of a stand mixer, place egg whites and sugar. Place over a pot or pan of simmering water and whisk constantly until sugar is dissolved. Check with your fingers to make sure there are no grains but be careful as mixture will be very hot.

Place bowl back on the stand mixer and using the whisk attachment, whisk for about 10 minutes or until soft, glossy peaks are formed and the bowl has reached room temperature.

Switch whisk attachment with the paddle attachment. Add in the butter one cube at a time to avoid lumps. Beat until all the butter has been incorporated and mixture is smooth. Add in the vanilla extract and salt and beat until smooth. Do not over mix.

Frost cooled cupcakes and top with sprinkles.

Enjoy!

2. Red Velvet Cupcakes With Cream Cheese Frosting

Light, fluffy and moist cupcakes with a beautiful red color topped with a delicious cream cheese frosting.

Makes: 12 cupcakes

Prep: 20 mins

Bake: 20 mins

Ingredients:

For the cupcakes:

- 4 tbsp. unsalted butter, softened
- ¾ cup white sugar
- 1 large egg
- 2½ tablespoons cocoa powder, preferably Dutch processed
- 2 ½ - 3 tbsp. red food coloring
- ½ tsp vanilla extract
- ½ cup buttermilk
- 1 cup flour
- ½ tsp salt
- ½ tsp baking soda
- 1 ½ tsp white vinegar

For the frosting:

- ½ cup unsalted butter, softened
- 1 ¾ cups icing sugar
- ⅛ tsp salt
- ½ tsp vanilla extract
- 1 cup cream cheese, cold and cut into cubes

Directions:

For the cupcakes:

Preheat the oven to 350°F and line a cupcake pan with 12 liners.

In a large bowl, whisk together the butter and sugar using a hand mixer, for about 4 minutes. Add in the egg and whisk on high until incorporated.

In a medium bowl, combine the cocoa powder, vanilla and red color. Add the mixture into the sugar mixture and whisk on high until combines. Scrape down the bowl and until the color is well incorporated and even.

Reduce speed to low and slowly add in a third of the buttermilk followed by a third of the flour. Scrape down the bowl and whisk on high until combined. Repeat process two more times until all the buttermilk and flour has been incorporated.

Reduce speed to low again and add in the baking soda, salt and white vinegar. Increase speed and beat on high for 2-3 minutes.

Pour batter into cupcake liners, filling the liners 2/3rd of the way up.

Bake for about 18-20 minutes or until a toothpick put into the centre of a cupcake comes out clean.

Cool cupcakes on a cooling rack.

For the frosting:

In the bowl of a stand mixer with a paddle attachment fitted, beat butter for a minute or so until creamy.

Add in the icing sugar, salt and vanilla and beat for about 6 minutes or until mixture has lightened.

Add in the cream cheese cubes one at a time, mixing well after each cube so no lumps are formed.

Beat for about 3 minutes until smooth and fluffy.

Frost cooled cupcakes.

Enjoy!

3. Cookies And Cream Cupcakes With Cream Frosting

Who doesn't love Oreos? These cookies and cream cupcakes are jam-packed full of Oreos and come with a cream frosting that contains (you guessed it) even more Oreos.

Makes: 12 cupcakes

Prep: 15 mins

Bake: 20 mins

Ingredients:

For the cupcakes:

- 1 1/2 cups all-purpose flour
- 1 tsp baking powder
- ¼ tsp salt
- 1 stick (113g) butter, room temperature
- ¾ cup white sugar
- 1 large egg + 1 egg white
- 1 ¼ tsp vanilla extract

- ½ cup milk
- 1 cup coarsely chopped Oreos

For the frosting:

- 2 egg whites
- ¾ cup white sugar
- ¾ cup unsalted butter, softened and cut into squares
- 1 tsp vanilla extract
- Pinch of salt
- 4 Oreos, chopped
- Mini Oreos, for decoration

Directions:

For the cupcakes:

Preheat the oven to 350°F and line a cupcake pan with 12 liners.

In a bowl, whisk together the dry ingredients. Set aside.

In the bowl of a stand mixer fitted with the paddle attachement or using a hand mixer, beat together the butter and sugar for 4 minutes. Add in eggs, one at a time, and beat until combined. Add in the vanilla and beat again.

Add in a third of the dry ingredients, followed by the a third of the milk. Repeat until all the flour and milk have been incorporated. Mix until just combined. Fold in the Oreos.

Pour batter into cupcake liners and bake for 15-18 minutes or until a toothpick put into the centre of a cupcake comes out clean (a few crumbs are fine too).

Cool cupcakes on a cooling rack.

For the frosting:

In the bowl of a stand mixer, place sugar and egg whites. Place bowl over a pan of simmering water and whisk until sugar is dissolved. Check with your fingers to make sure there are no grains but be careful as mixture will be very hot.

Place bowl back on the stand mixer and using the whisk attachment, whisk for about 10 minutes or until soft, glossy peaks are formed and the bowl has reached room temperature.

Switch whisk attachment with the paddle attachment. Add in the butter one cube at a time to avoid lumps. Beat until all the butter has been incorporated and mixture is smooth. Add in the vanilla extract and salt and beat until smooth. Do not over mix. Gently fold in the chopped Oreos.

Frost cooled cupcakes and top with mini Oreos.

Enjoy!

4. Sticky Toffee Cupcakes With Caramel Buttercream Frosting

Scrumptious sticky toffee cupcakes with a luscious caramel frosting.

Makes: 12 cupcakes

Prep: 40 mins

Bake: 20 mins

Ingredients:

For the cupcakes:

- 1 cup dates, pitted and chopped
- 1 tsp vanilla extract
- 1 ½ cup self-raising flour
- 1 tsp baking soda
- ¾ cup unsalted butter, softened
- ¾ cup cane sugar
- 2 large eggs, lightly beaten

For the frosting:

- 1 cup icing sugar
- 1/3 cup heavy cream
- 1/2 tsp salt
- 1 tsp vanilla extract
- 2 egg whites
- ¾ cup white sugar
- ¾ cup unsalted butter, softened and cut into squares
- Pinch of salt
- Toffees, to decorate

Directions:

For the cupcakes:

Preheat the oven to 350°F and line a cupcake pan with 12 liners.

In a large bowl, add ¾ cup boiling water to chopped dates and let soak for 25 minutes. Using a fork, break up the dates further and add in the vanilla extract.

In a small bowl, combine flour and baking soda and set aside.

In a large bowl, beat together butter and sugar for 3-4 minutes or until fluffy and light. Add in the eggs, one at a time, and beat until combined. Gently fold in the flour mixture, followed by the date mixture.

Pour batter into the cupcake liners and then bake for 15-18 minutes or until a toothpick put into the centre of a cupcake comes out clean.

Cool cupcakes on a cooling rack.

For the frosting:

In a small saucepan, add in the sugar and water (do not stir) and heat on high until mixture changes to an amber color, approximately 4-6 minutes. Remove from heat and carefully add in the cream, stirring constantly. Add in the vanilla and salt and stir until combined. Leave aside to cool and then refrigerate until needed.

In the bowl of a stand mixer, place egg whites and sugar. Place over a pot or pan of simmering water and whisk constantly until sugar is dissolved. Check with your fingers to make sure there are no grains but be careful as mixture will be very hot.

Place bowl back on the stand mixer and using the whisk attachment, whisk for about 10 minutes or until soft, glossy peaks are formed and the bowl has reached room temperature.

Switch whisk attachment with the paddle attachment. Add in the butter one cube at a time to avoid lumps. Beat until all the butter has been incorporated and mixture is smooth. Add in the vanilla extract and salt and beat until smooth. Do not over mix.

Add in cooled caramel and fold gently.

Frost cooled cupcakes and top with toffees.

Enjoy!

5. Carrot Cake And Cream Cheese Frosting

Moist carrot cake cupcakes with the most amazing cream cheese frosting recipe. With the addition of carrots, one might even call this healthy (Or not).

Makes: 12 cupcakes

Prep: 15 mins

Bake: 20 mins

Ingredients:

For the cupcakes:

- ½ cup white sugar
- ½ cup light brown sugar
- ¾ tsp salt
- ½ cup + 2 Tbsp vegetable oil
- 1 tsp vanilla extract
- 2 large eggs, room temperature
- 1 cup all-purpose flour
- 1 tsp baking soda
- 1 tsp ground cinnamon
- ¼ tsp ground nutmeg
- ¼ tsp ground ginger
- ¼ tsp ground cardamom
- 1/8 tsp ground cloves
- 1 ½ cups carrots, grated

For the frosting:

- ½ cup unsalted butter, softened
- 1 ¾ cups icing sugar
- ⅛ tsp salt
- ½ tsp vanilla extract
- 1 cup cream cheese, cold and cut into cubes

Directions:

For the cupcakes:

Preheat the oven to 350°F and line a cupcake pan with 12 liners.

In a medium sized bowl, combine the flour, baking soda and spices. Set aside.

In a large bowl, combine the white and brown sugar, salt, oil and vanilla extract until well combined. Add in the eggs, one at a time and whisk again.

Add in half of the flour mixture and whisk until combined. Add in the carrots and whisk again. Fold in the remaining flour mixture.

Pour batter into the cupcake liners and bake for 15-20 minutes or until a toothpick put into the centre of a cupcake comes out clean.

Cool cupcakes on a cooling rack.

For the frosting:

In the bowl of a stand mixer with a paddle attachment fitted, beat butter for a minute or so until creamy.

Add in the icing sugar, salt and vanilla and beat for about 6 minutes or until mixture has lightened.

Add in the cream cheese cubes one at a time, mixing well after each cube so no lumps are formed.

Beat for about 3 minutes until smooth and fluffy.

Frost cooled cupcakes.

Enjoy!

6. Raspberry Cupcakes With Swiss Meringue Buttercream Frosting

Light and fresh cupcakes that are a real treat in your mouth. Perfect for any occasion.

Makes: 12 cupcakes

Prep: 40 mins

Bake: 20 mins

Ingredients:

For the cupcakes:

- ¾ cup unsalted butter, softened
- ¾ cup + 2 Tbsp icing sugar
- 1 1/3 cup all-purpose flour
- 1 tsp baking powder
- 4 tbsp milk
- 2 large eggs
- 1 cup raspberries

For the buttercream:

- 2 egg whites
- ¾ cup white sugar
- ¾ cup unsalted butter, softened and cut into squares
- 1 tsp vanilla extract
- Pinch of salt
- Red food coloring
- 12 raspberries, for decoration

Directions:

For the cupcakes:

Preheat the oven to 350°F and line a cupcake pan with 12 liners.

In a food processor, add in all the ingredients except for the raspberries.

Drop one tablespoon of batter into the liners and top with 3 raspberries. Top again with another tablespoon.

Bake for 15-18 minutes or until a toothpick put into the centre of a cupcake comes out clean and the top is golden-brown.

Cool cupcakes on a cooling rack.

For the frosting:

In the bowl of a stand mixer, add the egg whites and sugar. Then place the bowl over a pan of simmering water and whisk until sugar is dissolved. Check with your fingers to make sure there are no grains but be careful as mixture will be very hot.

Place bowl back on the stand mixer and using the whisk attachment, whisk for about 10 minutes or until soft, glossy peaks are formed and the bowl has reached room temperature.

Switch whisk attachment with the paddle attachment. Add in the butter one cube at a time to avoid lumps. Beat until all the butter has been incorporated and mixture is smooth. Add in the vanilla extract and salt and beat until smooth. Do not over mix. Add in a drop of red food coloring and fold gently.

Frost cooled cupcakes and top with one raspberry each.

Enjoy!

7. Mocha Cupcakes With Cream Frosting

Coffee lovers rejoice! These moist and delicious cupcakes will make your house smell like a café!

Makes: 12 cupcakes

Prep: 20 mins

Bake: 20 mins

Ingredients:

For the cupcakes:

- 1/2 cup cocoa powder, preferably Dutch Processed
- ½ cup water, room temperature
- 1 cup white sugar
- 1/2 cup vegetable oil
- 2 eggs
- 1 ½ tsp vanilla extract
- 3/4 cup all-purpose flour
- ¾ tsp salt
- ½ tsp baking soda

For the frosting:

- 1 ½ cups heavy cream or whipping cream, cold
- 3 tbsp icing sugar
- 1 tbsp espresso powder
- 1 tsp vanilla extract
- Chocolate shavings, for decoration

Directions:

For the cupcakes:

Preheat the oven to 350°F and line a cupcake pan with 12 liners.

In a small bowl, combine flour, salt and baking powder. Set aside.

In a large bowl, whisk together the cocoa powder and water and let it sit for a minute or two. Add in the sugar, oil, eggs and vanilla extract and whish until well combined.

Add in the flour mixture and whisk until just combined.

Pour batter into the cupcake liners and bake for 15-20 minutes or until a toothpick put into the centre of a cupcake comes out clean.

Cool cupcakes on a cooling rack.

For the frosting:

In the bowl of a stand mixer fitted with the whisk attachment, whip together the cream, sugar, coffee powder and vanilla extract until stiff peaks form.

Frost cooled cupcakes and top with chocolate shavings, if desired.

Enjoy!

8. Lemon Cupcakes With Lemon Flavored Cream Cheese Frosting

Fluffy, moist and the perfect balance between sweet and tangy!

Makes: 12 cupcakes

Prep: 20 mins

Bake: 20 mins

Ingredients:

For the cupcakes:

- 1 1/3 cups all-purpose flour
- 1 tsp baking powder
- 1/4 tsp salt
- 1 cup white sugar
- 1 tbsp lemon zest
- 1 stick (113g) unsalted butter, softened to room temperature
- 2 eggs

- 1 tsp vanilla extract
- 6 tbsp milk
- 1 ½ tbsp freshly squeezed lemon juice

For the frosting:

- ½ cup unsalted butter, softened
- 1 ¾ cups icing sugar
- ⅛ tsp salt
- ½ tsp lemon zest
- ½ tsp freshly squeezed lemon juice
- 1 cup cream cheese, cold and cut into cubes

Directions:

For the cupcakes:

Preheat oven to 350°F and line a cupcake pan with 12 liners.

In a small bowl, combine sugar and zest.

In a medium bowl, combine baking powder, flour and salt. Set aside.

In a large bowl, using a hand mixer, beat butter and sugar for 4 minutes or until lightened in color and fluffy.

Add in the eggs, one at a time, followed by the vanilla extract and beat until well combined.

Lower the speed of the mixer and add in half of the dry mixture, followed by the lemon juice and milk. Add in the other half and beat until combined.

Pour batter into the cupcake liners and bake for 15-20 minutes or until a toothpick put into the centre of a cupcake comes out clean.

Cool cupcakes on a cooling rack.

For the frosting:

In the bowl of a stand mixer fitted with its paddle attachment, beat butter for a minute or so until creamy.

Add in the icing sugar, salt, lemon juice and zest and beat for about 6 minutes or until mixture has lightened.

Add in the cream cheese cubes one at a time, mixing well after each cube so no lumps are formed.

Beat for about 3 minutes until smooth and fluffy.

Frost cooled cupcakes.

Enjoy!

9. Chocolate Cupcakes With Ganache Frosting

These are quite possibly the best chocolate cupcakes in the world! Moist, rich and fudgy cupcakes with a smooth chocolatey ganache frosting.

Makes: 12 cupcakes

Prep: 25 mins

Bake: 20 mins

Ingredients:

For the cupcakes:

- 3/4 cup all-purpose flour
- 1/2 cup dark cocoa powder
- 1 tsp espresso powder
- 3/4 tsp baking powder
- 1/2 tsp baking soda
- 1/4 tsp salt
- 2 large eggs
- 1/2 cup white sugar
- 1/2 cup light brown sugar
- 1/3 cup vegetable oil
- 2 tsp vanilla extract
- 1/2 cup buttermilk

For the frosting:

- 5 oz dark chocolate chips
- 5 oz milk chocolate chips
- 10 oz heavy cream
- Chocolate shavings, for decoration

Directions:

For the cupcakes:

Preheat your oven to 350°F and line a cupcake pan along with 12 liners.

In a medium bowl, whisk the dry ingredients together and set aside.

In a large bowl, whisk the eggs, sugars, oil and vanilla until well combined and smooth. Add in half of the dry ingredients and then half of the buttermilk and whisk until just combined. Repeat with remaining dry mixture and buttermilk and stir until just combined.

Gently pour in the batter to cupcake liners and bake for 18-22 minutes or until a toothpick put into the centre of a cupcake comes out clean.

Set aside cupcakes to cool.

For the frosting:

In a large bowl, combine dark and milk chocolate chips.

In a medium-sized bowl, place cream and heat in the microwave until cream just starts to boil. Pour cream over the chocolate chips and let stand for 2 minutes.

Gently start whisking the mixture until smooth. Place in the refrigerator for about an hour or so.

Using a hand mixer, whip the ganache for 3-4 minutes until fluffy and light.

Frost cooled cupcakes and top with chocolate shavings.

Enjoy!

Recipe Notes: If the ganache is too firm when taken out of the refrigerator, heat if in the microwave for about 10-20 seconds and then begin whisking.

10. Tiramisu Cupcakes

These perfect Tiramisu cupcakes are soaked with a coffee syrup and topped off with the most luscious mascarpone frosting.

Makes: 12 cupcakes

Prep: 25 mins

Bake: 20 mins

Ingredients:

For the cupcakes:

- 1⅓ cups all-purpose flour
- 1 tsp baking powder
- 1 tsp espresso powder
- ¼ tsp salt
- 1 stick (113g) unsalted butter, softened
- ½ cup white sugar
- ½ cup brown sugar
- 2 large eggs
- 1 tsp vanilla extract
- ½ cup milk

For the coffee syrup:

- 1 tsp instant espresso powder dissolved in ¼ cup hot water
- 2 tbsp white sugar

For the frosting:

- ¾ cup mascarpone cheese
- ½ tbsp cornstarch
- ⅓ cup icing sugar
- 1 tsp espresso powder
- ¾ cup heavy cream, cold
- Cocoa powder, for dusting

Directions:

For the cupcakes:

Preheat the oven to 350°F and line a cupcake pan with 12 liners.

In a medium bowl, combine dry ingredients. Set aside.

In the bowl of a stand mixer fitted with the paddle attachment, beat butter and both sugars for about 4 minutes or until mixture is fluffy and light.

Add in the eggs, one at a time, followed by the vanilla extract and beat until well combined. Scrape down the bowl and beat again.

Lower the speed of the mixer and add in a third of the dry ingredients, beating until just combined. Add in half of the milk and beat again. Repeat process, ending with the last third of the dry ingredients, beating until combined.

Pour batter into the cupcake liners and bake for 18-20 minutes or until a toothpick put into the centre of a cupcake comes out clean.

Cool cupcakes on a cooling rack.

For the coffee syrup:

Combine the sugar and hot coffee mixture, mixing until well dissolved.

When cupcakes are relatively warm, brush evenly with coffee syrup. Set aside.

For the frosting:

In a large bowl, combine mascarpone cheese, corn starch, sugar and espresso powder. Set aside.

In the bowl of a stand mixer fitted with the whisk attachment, whisk cream for 2-4 minutes or until stiff peaks form. Gently fold in half the cream into the mascarpone cheese mixture. Fold in remaining half.

Frost cooled cupcakes and dust with cocoa powder.

Enjoy!

11. Coconut Cupcakes With Cream Cheese Frosting

Fluffy, moist and scrumptious, these coconut cupcakes are every coconut lover's dream!

Makes: 12 cupcakes

Prep: 15 mins

Bake: 25 mins

Ingredients:

For the cupcakes:

- 1 1/2 cups all-purpose flour
- 3/4 tsp. salt
- 1 3/4 tsp baking powder
- 2 sticks (227g) unsalted butter, softened
- 1 cup white sugar
- 1/2 cup full-fat coconut milk
- 2 large eggs
- 1 tsp. vanilla extract

- 1/2 cup unsweetened coconut flakes

For the frosting:

- ½ cup unsalted butter, softened
- 1 ¾ cups icing sugar
- ⅛ tsp. salt
- ½ tsp. coconut or vanilla extract
- 1 tbsp full-fat coconut milk
- 1 cup cream cheese, cold and cut into cubes

Directions:

For the cupcakes:

Preheat oven to 350°F and line a cupcake pan with 12 liners.

In a medium sized bowl, combine baking powder, flour and salt. Set aside.

In a small bowl, combine coconut milk and vanilla extract. Set aside.

In a large bowl, using a hand mixer, beat together sugar and butter for about 4 minutes or until fluffy and light. Add in the eggs, one at a time, and beat until well combined.

Add in 1/3rd of the flour mixture, followed by 1/3rd of the coconut milk mixture and beat until well combined. Repeat until all the dry ingredients and milk have been incorporated into the batter. Gently fold in the coconut flakes.

Pour batter into the liners and bake for 18-22 minutes or until a toothpick put into the centre of a cupcake comes out clean.

Cool cupcakes on a cooling rack.

For the frosting:

In the bowl of a stand mixer with a paddle attachment fitted, beat butter for a minute or so until creamy.

Add in the icing sugar, salt, coconut or vanilla extract and coconut milk and beat for about 6 minutes or until mixture has lightened.

Add in the cream cheese cubes one at a time, mixing well after each cube so no lumps are formed.

Beat for about 3 minutes until smooth and fluffy.

Frost cooled cupcakes.

Enjoy!

12. Matcha Cupcakes With Cream Frosting

These trendy and delicious cupcakes are perfect for all those tea drinkers out there!

Makes: 12 cupcakes

Prep: 15 mins

Bake: 20 mins

Ingredients:

For the cupcakes:

- 1 1/4 cups all-purpose flour
- 1/4 tsp salt
- 1/2 tsp baking soda
- 1 tsp baking powder
- 3/4 cup white sugar
- 1 ½ tbsp Matcha powder
- 3/4 cup buttermilk
- 1/2 cup vegetable oil
- 1 egg
- 1/2 tsp vanilla extract

For the frosting:

- 1 cup heavy cream or whipping cream, cold
- 1/2 tsp vanilla extract
- 1/4 cup icing sugar

Directions:

For the cupcakes:

Preheat the oven to 350°F and line a cupcake pan with 12 liners.

In a medium sized bowl, combine dry ingredients. Set aside.

In a large bowl, combine buttermilk, egg and vanilla extract, and whisk until well combined. Add in half of the flour mixture, whisking until just combined. Fold in the remaining half of the flour mixture.

Pour batter into the cupcake liners and bake for 15-18 minutes or until a toothpick put into the centre of a cupcake comes out clean.

Cool cupcakes on a cooling rack.

For the frosting:

In the bowl of a stand mixer with a whisk attachment fitted or using a hand mixer, whisk the cream, sugar and vanilla extract for 4 minutes or until stiff peaks form.

Frost cooled cupcakes and dust slightly with Matcha powder.

Enjoy!

13. Pumpkin Cupcakes With Cream Cheese Frosting

The best pumpkin cupcakes you'll ever eat! Celebrate the flavor of fall with these melt-in-your-mouth cupcakes that are topped off with classic cream cheese frosting.

Makes: 12 cupcakes

Prep: 25 mins

Bake: 20 mins

Ingredients:

For the cupcakes:

- 1 cup all-purpose flour
- ¾ cup white sugar
- 1 tsp baking powder
- 1 tsp ground cinnamon
- ½ tsp baking soda
- 2 eggs
- ½ cup vegetable oil
- 1 cup pumpkin puree, canned or homemade

For the frosting:

- ½ cup unsalted butter, softened
- 1 ¾ cups powdered sugar
- ⅛ tsp salt
- ½ tsp vanilla extract
- 1 cup cream cheese, cold and cut into cubes

Directions:

For the cupcakes:

Preheat the oven to 350°F and line a cupcake pan with 12 liners.

In a medium-sized bowl, combine flour, sugar, baking powder, baking soda and cinnamon. Set aside.

In a big bowl, mix eggs, oil and pumpkin puree. Add in the dry ingredients and whisk until well combined.

Pour batter into the liners and bake for 18-22 minutes or until a toothpick put into the centre of a cupcake comes out clean.

Cool cupcakes on a cooling rack.

For the frosting:

In the bowl of a stand mixer with a paddle attachment fitted, beat the butter for about 1 minute or so until creamy.

Add in the icing sugar, salt and vanilla and beat for about 6 minutes or until mixture has lightened.

Add in the cream cheese cubes one at a time, mixing well after each cube so no lumps are formed.

Beat for about 3 minutes until smooth and fluffy.

Frost cooled cupcakes.

Enjoy!

14. Black Forest Cupcakes With Cream Frosting

Moist, fluffy and rich chocolate cupcakes with a cherry jam filling and a whipped cream topping. So good!

Makes: 12 cupcakes

Prep: 20 mins

Bake: 20 mins

Ingredients:

For the cupcakes:

- 3/4 cup all-purpose flour
- 1/2 cup dark cocoa powder
- 1 tsp espresso powder
- 3/4 tsp baking powder
- 1/2 tsp baking soda
- 1/4 tsp salt
- 2 large eggs
- 1/2 cup white sugar
- 1/2 cup light brown sugar
- 1/3 cup vegetable oil
- 2 tsp vanilla extract
- 1/2 cup buttermilk

For the cherry filling:

- 1 ½ cup sweet cherries, pitted and chopped
- 3 tbsp white sugar
- 3 tbsp water
- 1 ½ tbsp corn starch
- 1 ½ tsp freshly squeezed lemon juice
- ¼ tsp vanilla extract

For the frosting:

- 1 cup heavy cream or whipping cream, cold
- 1/2 tsp vanilla extract
- 1/4 cup icing sugar
- 12 cherries, for decoration

Directions:

For the cupcakes:

Preheat oven to 350°F and line a cupcake pan with 12 liners.

In a medium bowl, combine the dry ingredients using a whisk. Set aside.

In a large bowl, combine the sugars, oil, eggs and vanilla extract and whisk until well combined and smooth. Add in half of the dry ingredients, followed by half of the buttermilk and whisk until just combined. Repeat with remaining dry ingredients and buttermilk and stir until just combined.

Pour batter into the liners and bake for 18-22 minutes or until a toothpick put into the centre of a cupcake comes out clean.

Cool cupcakes on a cooling rack.

For the cherry syrup:

In a medium-sized saucepan, combine cherries, sugar, lemon juice, water and corn starch, whisking until well combined. Heat mixture over medium heat until thickened. Remove from heat and add in the vanilla extract. Set aside to cool.

For the frosting:

In the bowl of a stand mixer with a whisk attachment fitted or you can simply use a hand mixer, whisk the cream, sugar and vanilla extract for 4 minutes or until stiff peaks form.

Once cupcakes and cherry filling are cooled, scoop out holes for the cherry filling from cupcake centres using a knife or a spoon. Divide cherry filling equally among cupcakes. Pipe on frosting and garnish each cupcake with a cherry on top.

Enjoy!

15. Chocolate Chip Cookie Dough Cupcakes With Ganache Frosting

Scrumptious cupcakes with a cookie dough centre that taste just like a freshly baked cookie! Don't forget your glass of milk.

Makes: 12 cupcakes

Prep: 25 mins

Bake: 20 mins

Ingredients:

For the cupcakes:

- 1 1/2 cup cake flour or all-purpose flour
- 2 tsp baking powder
- ¼ tsp salt
- 1 stick (113g) unsalted butter, softened
- 3/4 cup white sugar
- 2 tsp vanilla extract
- 2 large eggs
- 1/2 cup buttermilk

- 1/4 cup mini dark chocolate chips

For the cookie dough:

- 1 stick (113g) unsalted butter, softened
- 6 tbsp white sugar
- 6 tbsp brown sugar
- 2 tbsp milk
- ½ tbsp vanilla extract
- 1 ¼ cup all-purpose flour
- 1/8 tsp salt
- 1/2 cup mini dark chocolate chips

For the frosting:

- 5 oz dark chocolate chips
- 5 oz milk chocolate chips
- 10 oz heavy cream
- Mini cookies, for decoration

Directions:

For the cookie dough:

In a large bowl, using a hand mixer, beat the butter and sugars for 3 minutes or until fluffy and light. Add in milk and vanilla extract and beat until well combined.

Add in the flour and salt and beat until just combined. Gently fold in the chocolate chips.

Shape the cookie dough into 12 balls (approx. 1 tablespoon each) and place on a baking tray. Freeze overnight.

For the cupcakes:

Preheat the oven to 350°F and line a cupcake pan with 12 liners.

In a medium bowl, mix the baking powder, flour and salt. Set aside.

In the bowl of a stand mixer with the paddle attachment fitted or using a hand mixer, mix the white sugar, butter, and brown sugar and beat for about 4 minutes or until mixture is fluffy and light. Add in the eggs, one at a time, followed by the vanilla extract and beat until smooth.

Add in a third of the flour mixture followed by a third of the milk. Repeat process until all of the flour mixture and milk mixed in with the batter. Fold in chocolate chips.

Pour batter into the cupcake liners and drop a ball of cookie dough into the centre of each cupcake. Bake for 15-20 minutes or until a toothpick put into the centre of a cupcake comes out with a few moist cookie crumbs.

Cool cupcakes on a cooling rack.

For the ganache frosting:

In a large bowl, combine dark and milk chocolate chips.

In a medium-sized bowl, place cream and heat in the microwave until cream just starts to boil. Pour cream over the chocolate chips and let stand for 2 minutes.

Gently start whisking the mixture until smooth. Place in the refrigerator for about an hour or so.

Using a hand mixer, whip the ganache for 3-4 minutes until fluffy and light.

Frost cooled cupcakes and top with mini cookies.

Enjoy!

16. Dulce De Leche Cupcakes With Dulce De Leche Buttercream Frosting

Soft, sweet, caramel goodness! These Dulce de leche cupcakes are sure to be a hit among your friends and family.

Makes: 12 cupcakes

Prep: 15 mins

Bake: 20 mins

Ingredients:

For the dulse de leche cupcakes:

- 1 ½ cups all-purpose flour
- ½ tsp salt
- ¾ tsp baking powder
- 3/4 cup brown sugar
- 3/4 cup white sugar
- 1 stick (113g) unsalted butter, softened to room temperature
- 2 eggs

- 1 tsp vanilla extract
- ½ cup milk

For the frosting:

- 1 stick (113g) unsalted butter, room temperature
- 1 ½ cups icing sugar
- ¼ tsp salt
- ⅔ cup Dulce de leche
- 2 tbsp milk

Directions:

For the dulse de leche cupcakes:

Preheat oven to 350°F and line a cupcake pan with 12 liners.

In a small bowl, whisk dry ingredients.

In a large bowl, using a hand or stand mixer, whisk butter and both sugars for 4 minutes. Add in the eggs, one at a time, followed by the vanilla. Fold in the dry mixture, followed by the milk, until combined.

Pour batter into the liners and bake for 20 minutes or until a toothpick put into the centre of a cupcake turns out clean.

Cool cupcakes on a cooling rack.

For the frosting:

In the bowl of a stand mixer fixed with the paddle attachment or using a hand mixer, beat butter for 2 minutes. Add in the icing sugar, salt and Delce de leche and beat for 3 more minutes. Add in the milk, a tablespoon at a time, until the right consistency is achieved.

Frost cooled cupcakes.

Enjoy!

17. Birthday Cake Cupcakes With Buttercream Sprinkled Frosting

These sprinkled cupcakes are the perfect birthday gift! Moist, fluffy and colorful, what more can you ask for?

Makes: 12 cupcakes

Prep: 30 mins

Bake: 15 mins

Ingredients:

For the cupcakes:

- 1 ¼ cups all-purpose flour
- 1 cup white sugar
- 1 ½ baking powder
- ½ tsp salt
- ½ cup milk
- ¼ cup vegetable oil

- ½ tbsp vanilla extract
- 1 large egg
- ½ cup water
- ½ cup sprinkles

For the buttercream:

- 2 egg whites
- ¾ cup white sugar
- ¾ cup unsalted butter, softened and cut into squares
- 1 tsp vanilla extract
- Pinch of salt
- ¼ cup sprinkles + more for decoration

Directions:

For the cupcakes:

Preheat the oven to 350°F and line a cupcake pan with 12 liners.

In a large bowl, combine the dry ingredients with a fork or a whisk and set aside.

In a medium bowl, mix the milk, oil and vanilla. Add in the egg and whisk until well combined.

Add in the wet ingredients slowly to the dry ingredients and whisk until well combined.

Add in the water and whisk until smooth. Do not overmix. Fold in sprinkles.

Pour batter into cupcake liners, filling the liners half way up.

Bake for about 15 minutes or until a toothpick put into the centre of a cupcake comes out with a few crumbs.

Cool cupcakes on a cooling rack.

For the frosting:

In the bowl of a stand mixer, place egg whites and sugar. Place over a pot or pan of simmering water and whisk constantly until sugar is dissolved. Check with your fingers to make sure there are no grains but be careful as mixture will be very hot.

Place bowl back on the stand mixer and using the whisk attachment, whisk for about 10 minutes or until soft, glossy peaks are formed and the bowl has reached room temperature.

Switch whisk attachment with the paddle attachment. Add in the butter one cube at a time to avoid lumps. Beat until all the butter has been incorporated and mixture is smooth. Add in the vanilla extract and salt and beat until smooth. Do not over mix. Fold in sprinkles.

Frost cooled cupcakes and top with additional sprinkles.

Enjoy!

18. Gingerbread Cupcakes With Caramel Cream Cheese Frosting

Spice up your fall baking with these soft and sweet gingerbread cupcakes that are topped off with an amazing caramel cream cheese frosting that you will not be able to get enough of!

Makes: 12 cupcakes

Prep: 20 mins

Bake: 20 mins

Ingredients:

For the cupcakes:

- 1 ¼ cup all-purpose flour
- ½ tsp baking soda
- ½ tsp baking powder
- ½ tsp salt
- 1 1/2 tsp ground ginger
- 1 ½ tsp ground cinnamon
- 1/2 tsp ground nutmeg
- 1/4 tsp cloves
- 1 stick (113g) unsalted butter, softened
- 1/2 cup light brown sugar
- 1 egg
- 1 1/2 tsp vanilla extract
- 1/2 cup un-sulphured molasses
- 1/2 cup buttermilk

For the frosting:

- 1 stick (113g) unsalted butter, softened
- 1 ¾ cups icing sugar
- ⅛ tsp salt

- ½ tsp vanilla extract
- ¼ cup caramel sauce, homemade or store-bought
- 1 cup cream cheese, cold and cut into cubes

Directions:

For the cupcakes:

Preheat oven to 350°F and line a cupcake pan with 12 liners.

In a small bowl, combine dry ingredients. Set aside.

In another small bowl, combine the molasses and buttermilk. Set aside.

In the bowl of a stand mixer or using a hand mixer, beat the brown sugar and butter on the medium-high speed for 4 minutes. Add in the egg and beat until well combined.

Lower the speed of the mixer and add slowly add in the buttermilk mixture. Scrape down the bowl and beat until combined. Add in the dry ingredients and beat until just combined.

Pour batter into the cupcake liners and bake for 15-18 minutes or until a toothpick or knife inserted into the centre of a cupcake turns out clean.

Cool cupcakes on a cooling rack.

For the frosting:

In the bowl of a stand mixer, beat butter for a minute or so until creamy.

Add in the icing sugar, salt, vanilla and caramel sauce and beat for about 6 minutes or until mixture has lightened.

Add in the cream cheese cubes one at a time, mixing well after each cube so no lumps are formed.

Beat for about 3 minutes until smooth and fluffy.

Frost cooled cupcakes.

Enjoy!

19. Apple Pie Cupcakes With Cream Frosting

Skip the pie and try these apple pie cupcakes instead. They're perfectly spiced, fall-inspired cupcakes with a delicious apple pie filling topped off with a creamy, light frosting.

Makes: 12 cupcakes

Prep: 20 mins

Bake: 20 mins

Ingredients:

For the apple filling:

- 3 tbsp. white sugar
- 3 medium apples, peeled, cored and finely chopped
- 1 tbsp. freshly squeezed lemon juice

- 1/2 tsp. ground cinnamon
- 1/4 tsp. salt
- 2 tbsp. unsalted butter
- 2 tsp. all-purpose flour

For the cupcakes:

- 1 ½ cups all-purpose flour
- 1 ½ tsp. baking powder
- 1/4 tsp. salt
- 1 tsp. ground cinnamon
- 3/4 cup granulated sugar
- 2 large eggs
- 1 1/2 sticks (165g) unsalted butter, melted
- 2 tsp. vanilla extract
- ½ cup milk

For the frosting:

- 1 cup heavy cream, cold
- 1/2 tsp vanilla extract
- 1/4 cup icing sugar

Directions:

For the apple filling:

In a medium-sized bowl, combine chopped apples, sugar, lemon juice, cinnamon and salt.

In a medium saucepan, melt the butter over medium-high heat. Add in the apple mixture and cook for 5-7 minutes or until apples are soft and tender. Add in the flour and stir until thickened.

Let the mixture cool completely.

For the cupcakes:

In a medium-sized bowl, combine dry ingredients.

In the bowl of a stand mixer with a paddle attachment fitted or using a hand mixer, beat sugar and eggs for 2-3 minutes or until pale and creamy. Add in the melted butter slowly, followed by the vanilla extract. Add in half of the flour mixture, followed by half of the milk. Repeat until batter is smooth.

Pour batter into the cupcake liners and add in a spoonful or so of the apple filling into the centre of each cupcake. Bake for 20 minutes or until a toothpick inserted along the edge of a cupcake comes out clean.

Cool cupcakes on a cooling rack.

For the frosting:

In the bowl of a stand mixer fitted with a whisk attachment or using a hand mixer, whisk the cream, sugar and vanilla extract for 4 minutes or until stiff peaks form.

Frost cooled cupcakes and dust slightly with cinnamon, if desired.

Enjoy!

20. Nutella Cupcakes With Nutella Frosting

Soft and fudgy chocolate cupcakes filled with Nutella sauce and topped off with a smooth luscious Nutella frosting, these dangerously addictive cupcakes might just become your favourite thing to eat in the whole world!

Makes: 12 cupcakes

Prep: 25 mins

Bake: 20 mins

Ingredients:

For the cupcakes:

- 3/4 cup all-purpose flour
- 1/2 cup dark cocoa powder
- 1 tsp espresso powder
- 3/4 tsp baking powder
- 1/2 tsp baking soda
- 1/4 tsp salt
- 2 large eggs
- 1/2 cup white sugar
- 1/2 cup light brown sugar
- 1/3 cup vegetable oil
- 2 tsp vanilla extract
- 1/2 cup buttermilk

For the Nutella sauce:
- 3 tbsp Nutella
- 2 tbsp milk

For the frosting:
- 1 stick unsalted butter, softened
- ½ stick (54g) cream cheese, softened but cool and cut into squares
- ¾ cup Nutella
- 4 oz semisweet chocolate chips

Directions:

For the cupcakes:

Preheat the oven to 350°F and line a cupcake pan with 12 liners.

In a medium bowl, whisk the dry ingredients.

In a large bowl, combine the eggs, sugars, oil and vanilla extract and whisk until well combined and smooth. Add in 1/2 of the dry ingredients, followed by 1/2 of the buttermilk and whisk until just combined. Repeat with remaining dry mixture and buttermilk and stir until just combined.

Pour batter into the liners and bake for 18-22 minutes or until a toothpick put into the centre of a cupcake comes out clean.

Cool cupcakes on a cooling rack.

For the Nutella sauce:

In a small bowl, whisk together Nutella and milk until smooth. Set aside.

For the Nutella frosting:

In a medium-sized microwave-safe bowl, melt chocolate chips in 20 second intervals. Set aside to cool.

In a large bowl, using a hand mixer, beat butter for about a minute or until smooth and creamy. Add in the cream cheese, one cube at a time, and beat until smooth. Add in the Nutella and beat for a minute and then add in the cooled, melted chocolate. Beat for about a minute or more or until combined.

Once cupcakes are cooled, scoop out holes for the Nutella sauce from cupcake centres using a knife or a spoon. Pour in the sauce all ¾th of the way and then frost cupcakes with Nutella frosting.

Enjoy!

21. Peanut Butter Cupcakes With Ganache Frosting

The ultimate dessert for peanut butter lovers! Fluffy, moist peanut butter cupcakes topped off with chocolate ganache, this is a match made in heaven.

Makes: 12 cupcakes

Prep: 1 hr

Bake: 20 mins

Ingredients:

For the cupcakes:

- 1 cup + 2 tbsp all-purpose flour
- 1 ½ tsp baking powder
- 1/4 + 1/8 tsp baking soda
- 1/4 tsp salt
- ¼ cup vegetable oil
- ¾ cup brown sugar
- 2 eggs
- 1 ½ tsp vanilla extract
- 1/4 cup peanut butter
- 6 tbsp milk

For the frosting:

- 5 oz dark chocolate chips
- 5 oz milk chocolate chips
- 10 oz heavy cream
- Mini peanut butter cups, for topping

Directions:

For the cupcakes:

Preheat oven to 350°F and line a cupcake pan with 12 liners.

In a small bowl, combine dry ingredients and set aside.

In a large bowl, whisk oil and sugar until combined. Add in eggs, one at a time, followed by the vanilla extract and whisk until smooth. Add in peanut butter and whisk again.

Slowly add in 1/3rd of the flour mixture followed by 1/3rd of the milk. Repeat until all of the dry ingredients and milk are added in the batter. Whisk until just combined.

Pour batter into the liners and bake for 18-22 minutes or until a toothpick put into the centre of a cupcake comes out clean.

Cool cupcakes on a cooling rack.

For the frosting:

In a large bowl, combine dark and milk chocolate chips.

In a medium-sized bowl, place cream and heat in the microwave until cream just starts to boil. Pour cream over the chocolate chips and let stand for 2 minutes.

Gently start whisking the mixture until smooth. Place in the refrigerator for about an hour or so.

Using a hand mixer, whip the ganache for 3-4 minutes until fluffy and light.

Frost cooled cupcakes and top mini peanut butter cups.

Enjoy!

22. Rafaello Cupcakes With Rafaello Cream Cheese Frosting

Delicious almond and coconut flavored cupcakes topped off with coconut cream cheese frosting and Rafaellos, these cupcakes are truly a decadent treat.

Makes: 12 cupcakes

Prep: 15 mins

Bake: 15 mins

Ingredients:

For the cupcakes:

- 1 ¼ cups all-purpose flour
- 1 cup white sugar
- 1 ½ baking powder
- ½ tsp salt
- ½ cup milk
- ¼ cup vegetable oil
- 1 tsp coconut extract
- ½ tsp almond extract
- 1 large egg
- ½ cup water
- ¼ cup sweetened coconut flakes

For the frosting:

- ½ cup unsalted butter, softened
- 1 ¾ cups icing sugar
- ⅛ tsp salt
- ½ tsp coconut extract
- 1 cup cream cheese, cold and cut into cubes
- 3 tbsp sweetened coconut flakes
- 12 Rafaellos, for decoration

Directions:

For the cupcakes:

Preheat the oven to 350°F and line a cupcake pan with 12 liners.

In a large bowl, combine the dry ingredients with a fork or a whisk and set aside.

In a medium bowl, combine the milk, oil, coconut extract and almond extract. Add in the egg and whisk until well combined.

Slowly add in the wet ingredients to the dry ingredients and whisk until well combined.

Add in the water and whisk until smooth. Do not overmix. Fold in coconut flakes.

Pour batter into cupcake liners, filling the liners half way up.

Bake for about 15 minutes or until a toothpick put into the centre of a cupcake comes out clean.

Cool cupcakes on a cooling rack.

For the frosting:

In the bowl of a stand mixer with a paddle attachment fitted, beat butter for a minute or so until creamy.

Add in the icing sugar, salt and coconut extract and beat for about 6 minutes or until mixture has lightened.

Add in the cream cheese cubes one at a time, mixing well after each cube so no lumps are formed.

Beat for about 3 minutes until smooth and fluffy. Fold in the coconut flakes.

Frost cooled cupcakes and top with Rafaellos.

Enjoy!

23. Lotus Biscoff Cupcakes With Cream Frosting

If you're in love with lotus biscoff (speculoos) cookies, just like everyone else is, you are going to love these cupcake! Sweet, moist and creamy and topped off with a cream frosting to balance out the sweetness.

Makes: 12 cupcakes

Prep: 15 mins

Bake: 15 mins

Ingredients:

For the cupcakes:

- 1 ½ cups all-purpose flour
- 1 ½ cups white sugar
- ¼ + 1/8 tsp ground cinnamon
- 3 tbsp Lotus Biscoff or cookie butter spread
- ¾ tsp baking soda
- ½ cup + 1 tbsp buttermilk
- 2 large eggs
- 1 ½ tsp vanilla extract

For the frosting:

- 1 ¾ cups + 2 tbsp heavy cream
- 2 tbsp whipping cream
- ¼ cup icing sugar
- 2 tbsp cream cheese
- 3 crushed Lotus biscoff cookies
- 12 Lotus biscoff cookies, for decoration

For the frosting:

- 1 cup heavy cream or whipping cream, cold
- 1/2 tsp vanilla extract
- 1/4 cup icing sugar
- 12 Lotus cookies

Directions:

For the cupcakes:

Preheat the oven to 350°F and line a cupcake pan with 12 liners.

In a medium-sized bowl, combine dry ingredients. Set aside.

In a large bowl, using a hand mixer, whisk together butter and sugar for 3 minutes or until pale and fluffy. Add in the eggs, one at a time, followed by the vanilla extract and beat until well combined. Add in the cookie spread and whisk again.

Add in 1/3rd of the dry ingredients followed by 1/3rd of the buttermilk. Repeat until all the dry ingredients and milk are in the batter.

Bake for about 15 minutes or until a toothpick put into the centre of a cupcake comes out clean.

Cool cupcakes on a cooling rack.

For the frosting:

In the bowl of a stand mixer fitted with a whisk attachment or using a hand mixer, whisk the cream, sugar and vanilla extract for 4 minutes or until stiff peaks form.

Frost cooled cupcakes and top each with a Lotus cookie.

Enjoy!

24. Banana Cupcakes With Brown Butter Cream Cheese Frosting

Put those ripe bananas to good use by making these melt-in-your-mouth moist banana bread cupcakes with an insanely delicious browned butter cream cheese frosting.

Makes: 12 cupcakes

Prep: 45 mins

Bake: 20 mins

Ingredients:

For the cupcakes:

- 1 cup plus 2 tablespoons all-purpose flour
- 1/2 tsp baking powder
- 1/2 tsp baking soda
- 1/4 tsp salt
- 1 stick (113g) unsalted butter, softened
- 1/4 cup white sugar
- 1/4 cup brown sugar
- 1/4 cup sour cream or yogurt
- 2 tsp vanilla extract
- 2 large eggs
- 2 large or 3 small-medium ripe bananas, peeled, and mashed
- ¼ cup semi-sweet chocolate chips, coated in flour

For the frosting:

- ½ cup unsalted butter, softened
- 1 ¾ cups icing sugar
- ⅛ tsp salt
- ½ tsp vanilla extract
- 1 cup cream cheese, cold and cut into cubes

Directions:

For the cupcakes:

Preheat oven to 350°F and line a cupcake pan with 12 liners.

In a medium-sized bowl, combine dry ingredients. Set aside.

In a large bowl, using a hand mixer, beat butter and both sugars for 3-4 minutes or until pale. Add in the eggs, one at a time, followed by the vanilla extract and sour cream or yogurt and beat until well combined.

Slowly add in the dry mixture and beat until combined. Fold in the mashed banana and chocolate chips.

Pour batter into the cupcake liners and then bake for about 20 minutes or until a toothpick put into the centre of a cupcake comes out clean.

Cool cupcakes on a cooling rack.

For the frosting:

In a medium-sized saucepan, melt butter over medium-high heat. Reduce heat and cook until the butter changes into an amber color, stirring constantly.

Remove from heat, cover and cool in the freezer for about 30 minutes or until butter is solid but still soft.

In the bowl of a stand mixer with a paddle attachment fitted, beat butter for a minute or so until creamy.

Add in the icing sugar, salt and vanilla and beat for about 6 minutes or until mixture has lightened.

Add in the cream cheese cubes one at a time, mixing well after each cube so no lumps are formed.

Beat for about 3 minutes until smooth and fluffy.

Frost cooled cupcakes.

Enjoy!

25. Hummingbird Cupcakes With Cream Cheese Frosting

Soft, fluffy, fruity and nutty, these cupcakes are a Southern classic joy guaranteed to please everyone!

Makes: 12 cupcakes

Prep: 15 mins

Bake: 20 mins

Ingredients:

For the cupcakes:

- 1 1/2 cups all-purpose flour
- 3/4 cup white sugar
- 1/2 tsp baking soda
- 1/2 tsp ground cinnamon
- 1/4 tsp salt
- 1/4 tsp ground cardamom
- 1 large egg
- 1/4 cup unsweetened applesauce

- 1 1/2 vegetable oil
- 2 large or 3 small-medium bananas, peeled and mashed
- 4 ounces crushed pineapple, undrained
- 1 tsp vanilla extract
- 1/2 cup chopped pecans

For the frosting:

- ½ cup unsalted butter, softened
- 1 ¾ cups icing sugar
- ⅛ tsp salt
- ½ tsp vanilla extract
- 1 cup cream cheese, cold and cut into cubes
- Chopped pecans, for decoration

Directions:

For the cupcakes:

Preheat the oven to 350°F and line a cupcake pan with 12 liners.

In a medium-sized bowl, combine dry ingredients. Set aside.

In a large bowl, combine applesauce, oil, bananas, pineapple and vanilla extract. Add in the egg and whisk until smooth. Add in the dry ingredients and whisk until just combined. Fold in chopped pecans.

Pour batter into the liners and bake for 18-22 minutes or until a toothpick put into the centre of a cupcake comes out clean.

Cool cupcakes on a cooling rack.

For the frosting:

In a large bowl, using a hand mixer, beat butter for a minute or so until creamy.

Add in the icing sugar, salt and vanilla and beat for about 6 minutes or until mixture has lightened.

Add in the cream cheese cubes one at a time, mixing well after each cube so no lumps are formed.

Beat for about 3 minutes until smooth and fluffy.

Frost cooled cupcakes and top with chopped pecans.

Enjoy!

26. Strawberry Cheesecake Cupcakes With Cream Cheese Frosting

Delicious and moist strawberry cupcakes with a graham cracker crust and a cream cheese topping, these cupcakes are perfect for cheesecake lovers!

Makes: 12 cupcakes

Prep: 25 mins

Bake: 20 mins

Ingredients:

For the crust:

- 3/4 cup graham cracker or digestive biscuit crumbs
- 1 tbsp white sugar
- 2 tbsp unsalted butter, melted

For the cupcakes:

- 1 teaspoon baking powder
- 1/4 tsp salt
- 1 1/2 cups all-purpose flour
- 1 stick (113g) unsalted butter, softened
- 1 cup white sugar
- 2 large eggs
- ¾ cup fresh strawberries, chopped and pureed
- ¼ cup milk
- 1 tsp vanilla extract

For the frosting:

- ½ cup unsalted butter, softened
- 1 ¾ cups icing sugar
- ⅛ tsp salt
- ½ tsp vanilla extract
- 1 cup cream cheese, cold and cut into cubes
- Additional graham cracker or digestive biscuits crumbs, for decoration
- 12 strawberries, for decoration

Directions:

For the crust:

Preheat oven to 350°F and line a cupcake pan with 12 liners.

In a small bowl, combine graham cracker crumbs, sugar and melted butter. Spoon evenly into cupcake liners and press down with a spoon.

Bake for 5 minutes.

Remove from oven and set aside.

For the cupcakes:

In a medium-sized bowl, combine dry ingredients.

In the bowl of a stand mixer or using a hand mixer, beat butter and sugar for 4 minutes or until lightened in color and fluffy. Add in the eggs, one at a time, and beat until combined. Add in the strawberries, milk and vanilla extract and beat until combined.

Add in the dry ingredients and beat until just combined.

Pour batter into the liners and bake for 18-22 minutes or until a toothpick put into the centre of a cupcake comes out clean.

Cool cupcakes on a cooling rack.

For the frosting:

In a large bowl, using a hand mixer, beat butter for a minute or so until creamy.

Add in the icing sugar, salt and vanilla and beat for about 6 minutes or until mixture has lightened.

Add in the cream cheese cubes one at a time, mixing well after each cube so no lumps are formed.

Beat for about 3 minutes until smooth and fluffy.

Frost cooled cupcakes and top with chopped pecans.

Enjoy!

27. Peaches And Cream Cupcakes

Light, fresh and tangy, these are the perfect cupcakes for summer.

Makes: 12 cupcakes

Prep: 15 mins

Bake: 20 mins

Ingredients:

For the peach cupcakes:

- ¼ tsp baking soda
- 1 tsp cinnamon
- ½ tsp salt
- 1 tsp baking powder
- 1/2 cup white sugar
- 1 2/3 cups all-purpose flour
- 1/2 cup brown sugar
- 1 ½ stick (165g) unsalted butter, softened
- 3 egg whites

- 2 tsp vanilla extract
- 1/4 cup + 2 tbsp yogurt
- 1/2 cup milk
- 3/4 cup fresh peaches, chopped

For the frosting:

- 1 cup heavy cream, cold
- 1/2 tsp vanilla extract
- 1/4 cup icing sugar
- 12 peach slices, for decoration

Directions:

For the peach cupcakes:

Preheat the oven to 350°F and line a cupcake pan with 12 liners.

In the bowl of a stand mixer fitted with the whisk attachment or using a hand mixer, combine flour, sugars, baking powder, baking soda and salt.

Add in the butter and whisk until combined. Slowly add in the egg whites, vanilla extract, yogurt and milk and whisk on medium-high speed until well combined. Gently fold in the peaches.

Pour batter into the liners and bake for 18-22 minutes or until a toothpick put into the centre of a cupcake comes out clean.

Cool cupcakes on a cooling rack.

For the frosting:

In the bowl of a stand mixer with a whisk attachment fitted or using a hand mixer, whisk the cream, sugar and vanilla extract for 4 minutes or until stiff peaks form.

Frost cooled cupcakes and top with peach slices.

Enjoy!

28. Salted Caramel Cupcakes With Caramel Buttercream Frosting

Heavenly caramel cupcakes with a hint of salt and topped with a luscious caramel buttercream frosting.

Makes: 12 cupcakes

Prep: 25 mins

Bake: 20 mins

Ingredients:

For the cupcakes:

- 1 tsp baking powder
- ½ tsp baking soda
- ½ tsp salt
- ½ tsp ground cinnamon
- 2 cups all-purpose flour

- 1/2 cup whole milk
- 1/2 cup yogurt or sour-cream
- 1 stick (113 g) unsalted butter, softened
- 1/4 cup white sugar
- 3/4 cup brown sugar
- 2 large eggs plus one large egg yolk,
- 1/4 cup boiling hot water

For the frosting:

- 1 cup icing sugar
- 1/3 cup heavy cream
- 1/2 tsp salt
- 1 tsp vanilla extract
- 2 egg whites
- ¾ cup white sugar
- ¾ cup unsalted butter, softened and cut into squares
- Pinch of salt

Directions:

For the cupcakes:

Preheat the oven to 350°F and line a cupcake pan with 12 liners.

In a small bowl, combine milk and yogurt or sour cream. Set aside.

In a medium-sized bowl, combine the dry ingredients. Set aside.

In the bowl of a stand mixer with the paddle attachment fitted or using a hand mixer, beat butter and sugars for 4 minutes or until pale and fluffy. Add in the eggs, one at a time, followed by the egg yolk. Beat until combined. Slowly add in a third of the flour mixture followed by half of the milk mixture. Repeat until all of the flour mixture and milk mixture are added into the batter.

Slowly stream in the hot water and mix until just combined.

Pour batter into the cupcake liners and bake for 18-20 minutes or until a toothpick put into the centre of a cupcake comes out clean.

Cool cupcakes on a cooling rack.

For the frosting:

In a small saucepan, add in the sugar and water (do not stir) and heat on high until mixture changes to an amber color, approximately 4-6 minutes. Remove from heat and carefully add in the cream, stirring constantly. Add in the vanilla and salt and stir until combined. Leave aside to cool and then refrigerate until needed.

In the bowl of a stand mixer, place egg whites and sugar. Place over a pot or pan of simmering water and whisk constantly until sugar is dissolved. Check with your fingers to make sure there are no grains but be careful as mixture will be very hot.

Place bowl back on the stand mixer and using the whisk attachment, whisk for about 10 minutes or until soft, glossy peaks are formed and the bowl has reached room temperature.

Switch whisk attachment with the paddle attachment. Add in the butter one cube at a time to avoid lumps. Beat until all the butter has been incorporated and mixture is smooth. Add in the vanilla extract and salt and beat until smooth. Do not over mix.

Add in cooled caramel and fold gently.

Frost cooled cupcakes.

Enjoy!

29. Blueberry Cupcakes With White Chocolate Blueberry Buttercream Frosting

Fluffy and fresh blueberry cupcakes with the perfect blueberry frosting. The perfectly well-balanced flavor bomb!

Makes: 12 cupcakes

Prep: 20 mins

Bake: 20 mins

Ingredients:

For the cupcakes:

- 1 2/3 cups all-purpose flour
- Pinch of salt
- 1 tsp baking powder
- 1 tsp baking soda
- 1 3/4 stick (195g) unsalted butter, softened

- 1 cup white sugar
- 2 tsp vanilla extract
- 3 eggs
- 4 tbsp milk
- 1 cup fresh blueberries, tossed in flour

For the frosting:

- 2 sticks (227g) unsalted butter, softened
- 12 ounces white chocolate, chopped
- 1 cup icing sugar
- 1 tsp vanilla extract
- 12 blueberries, for topping

Directions:

For the cupcakes:

Preheat the oven to 350°F and line a cupcake pan with 12 liners.

In a medium-sized bowl, combine dry ingredients.

In a large bowl, using a hand mixer, beat butter and sugar for 4 minutes. Add in the eggs, vanilla extract and milk and beat until combined.

Add in the dry mixture and beat until just combined. Fold in the flour-coated blueberries.

Pour batter into the liners and bake for 18-22 minutes or until a toothpick put into the centre of a cupcake comes out clean.

Cool cupcakes on a cooling rack.

For the frosting:

In a microwave-safe bowl, melt white chocolate in 20 second intervals until smooth. Set aside to cool.

In a large bowl, using a hand mixer, beat butter for 1 minute or until creamy. Add in the icing sugar, and vanilla extract and beat for 1 more minute. Add in the melted white chocolate and beat for 1 minute or until frosting is fluffy and light.

Frost cooled cupcakes and top with a blueberry each.

Enjoy!

30. Orange Cupcakes With Cream Frosting

Light, fresh and tender cupcakes teeming with orange flavor and topped off with a light whipped cream frosting.

Makes: 12 cupcakes

Prep: 20 mins

Bake: 15 mins

Ingredients:

For the cupcakes:

- 1½ cups all-purpose flour

- 1 tsp baking powder
- ½ tsp salt
- ½ tsp baking soda
- 1 stick (113g) unsalted butter, softened
- ¾ cups white sugar
- Zest of 1 orange
- 2 eggs
- 1 tsp orange extract, optional
- ½ cup yogurt or sour cream
- ¼ cup freshly squeezed orange juice

For the frosting:

- 1 cup heavy cream, cold
- 1/2 tsp vanilla extract
- 1/4 cup icing sugar

Directions:

For the cupcakes:

Preheat oven to 350°F and line a cupcake pan with 12 liners.

In a small bowl, combine orange juice and yogurt or sour cream. Set aside.

In a medium-sized bowl, combine dry ingredients. Set aside.

In the bowl of a stand mixer with a paddle attachment fitted or using a hand mixer, beat butter and sugar for 4 minutes. Add in the eggs, one at a time, followed by the orange zest and orange extract (if using) and beat until well combined.

Add in half of the flour mixture followed by half of the orange juice mixture. Repeat process and beat until well combined.

Pour batter into the cupcake liners and bake for 12-15 minutes or until a toothpick put into the centre of a cupcake comes out clean.

Cool cupcakes on a cooling rack.

For the frosting:

In a large bowl, using a hand mixer, whisk the cream, sugar and vanilla extract for 4 minutes or until stiff peaks form.

Once cupcakes and cherry filling are cooled, scoop out holes for the cherry filling from cupcake centres using a knife or a spoon. Divide cherry filling equally among cupcakes. Pipe on frosting and garnish each cupcake with a cherry on top.

Enjoy!

Conclusion

So there you have it! 30 of the most moist, fluffy and flavorful cupcake recipes. I sincerely hope you give all of the recipes a try because you never know what flavor may turn into your new favourite. Cupcakes also make an amazing gift so be sure to share these treats with friends, family and co-workers.

And again, for the final time, enjoy!

Part 2

Introduction

All recipes are for 24 cupcakes, so choose 2 12-cup cupcake tins or one 24-cup cupcake or muffin tin. After lining the tins, fill 2/3 of the cup, not more.

Once the cupcakes are baked, you can use apple corer and get the middle section out to make a hole for the filling. None of the recipes are mentioning the cupcake filling and all I can say is that after years of experimenting, my kids said that they prefer fruit preserve cupcake fillings over creamy ones. Their favorite ones are homemade apricot preserve followed by homemade plum, apple, quince and any berries preserve. Enjoy!!!

Cupcakes Recipes

Double Vanilla Cupcakes

Yields 24 cupcakes

Vanilla Cupcakes Ingredients:

1 cup cake flour

1 cup all-purpose flour

1 cup sugar

1 + 1/2 tsp. baking powder

1/2 tsp. table salt

1 stick chopped unsalted butter at room temperature

3/4 cup milk

2 large eggs

1/2 tsp. salt

1 + 1/2 tsp. vanilla extract

Buttercream Vanilla Frosting Ingredients:

2 sticks chopped unsalted butter at room temperature

3 cups powdered sugar

1 tsp. vanilla extract

Baking Instructions: Preheat oven to 375f and line muffin cups. Beat butter and sugar until light and fluffy and beat in eggs one at a time. Mix all dry ingredients in fairly large mixing bowl. Add dry ingredients alternating with milk. Add vanilla at the end. Divide evenly among pans and bake for 18-24 minutes and let cool in pans.

Buttercream Instructions:

Beat the butter for few minutes and start adding sugar until light and fluffy and mix in vanilla until incorporated. Frost the cupcakes and decorate with melted chocolate drizzles and sprinkles.

Vanilla & Cranberry Cream Cupcakes

Yields 24 cupcakes

Vanilla Cupcakes Ingredients:

1 cup cake flour

1 cup all-purpose flour

1 cup sugar

1 + 1/2 tsp. baking powder

1/2 tsp. table salt

1 stick chopped unsalted butter at room temperature

3/4 cup buttermilk

2 large eggs

1/2 tsp. salt

1 + 1/2 tsp. vanilla extract

2 Tbsp. chopped dried cranberries

Buttercream Frosting Ingredients:

2 sticks chopped unsalted butter at room temperature

3 cups powdered sugar

1/4 cup canned cranberry sauce

1 tsp. vanilla extract

Baking Instructions: Preheat oven to 375f and line muffin cups. Beat butter and sugar until light and fluffy and beat in eggs one at a time. Mix all dry ingredients in fairly large mixing bowl. Add dry ingredients alternating with buttermilk. Add vanilla at the end. Divide evenly among pans and bake for 18-24 minutes and let cool in pans.

Buttercream Instructions:

Beat the butter for few minutes and start adding sugar until light and fluffy and mix in vanilla and cranberry sauce until incorporated. Frost the cupcakes and decorate with melted chocolate and sprinkles.

Vanilla & Blueberry Cupcakes

Yields 24 cupcakes

Vanilla Cupcakes Ingredients:

1 cup cake flour

1 cup all-purpose flour

1 cup sugar

1 + 1/2 tsp. baking powder

1/2 tsp. table salt

1 stick chopped unsalted butter at room temperature

3/4 cup Greek Yogurt

2 large eggs

1/2 tsp. salt

1 + 1/2 tsp. vanilla extract

1/4 cup blueberries

Buttercream Frosting Ingredients:

2 sticks chopped unsalted butter at room temperature

3 cups powdered sugar

1/4 cup blueberry preserve

1 tsp. vanilla extract

Baking Instructions: Preheat oven to 375f and line muffin cups. Beat butter and sugar until light and fluffy and beat in eggs one at a time. Mix all dry ingredients in fairly large mixing bowl. Add dry ingredients alternating with yogurt. Add vanilla and blueberries at the end. Divide evenly among pans and bake for 18-24 minutes and let cool in pans.

Buttercream Instructions:

Beat the butter for few minutes and start adding sugar until light and fluffy and mix in vanilla and blueberry preserve until incorporated. Frost the cupcakes and decorate with sugar frosting and sprinkles.

Chocolate & Butter Cream Cupcakes

Yields 24 cupcakes

Chocolate Cupcakes Ingredients:

1 cup cake flour

1 cup all-purpose flour

1 cup sugar

1/2 cup melted dark chocolate

3/4 cup cocoa powder, unsweetened

1 + 1/2 tsp. baking powder

1/2 tsp. table salt

1 stick chopped unsalted butter at room temperature

3/4 cup hot coffee

2 large eggs

1/2 tsp. salt

1 + 1/2 tsp. vanilla extract

Buttercream Frosting Ingredients:

2 sticks chopped unsalted butter at room temperature

3 cups powdered sugar

1 tsp. vanilla extract

Baking Instructions: Preheat oven to 375f and line muffin cups. Beat butter and sugar until light and fluffy and beat in eggs one at a time. Mix all dry ingredients in fairly large mixing bowl. Add dry ingredients alternating with coffee. Add vanilla at the end. Divide evenly among pans and bake for 18-24 minutes and let cool in pans.

Buttercream Instructions:

Beat the butter for few minutes and start adding sugar until light and fluffy and mix in vanilla until incorporated. Frost the cupcakes and decorate with chocolate shavings.

Brown Sugar Cupcakes

Yields 24 cupcakes

Vanilla Cupcakes Ingredients:

1 cup cake flour

1 cup all-purpose flour

1 cup brown sugar

1 + 1/2 tsp. baking powder

1/2 tsp. table salt

1 stick chopped unsalted butter at room temperature

3/4 cup milk

2 large eggs

1/2 tsp. salt

1 + 1/2 tsp. vanilla extract

2 Tbsp. ground walnuts

Buttercream Frosting Ingredients:

2 sticks chopped unsalted butter at room temperature

1 cup powdered brown sugar

1 tsp. vanilla extract

Baking Instructions: Preheat oven to 375f and line muffin cups. Beat butter and sugar until light and fluffy and beat in eggs one at a time. Mix all dry ingredients in fairly large mixing bowl. Add dry ingredients alternating with milk. Add vanilla and walnuts at the end. Divide evenly among pans and bake for 18-24 minutes and let cool in pans.

Buttercream Instructions:
Spread brown sugar in the pan for few hours (it has to be dry before processing). Put it in the food processor and process it until you get a brown sugar powder. Beat the butter for few minutes and start adding sugar until light and fluffy and mix in vanilla until incorporated.

Blackberry & Raspberry Cream Cupcakes

Yields 24 cupcakes

Vanilla Cupcakes Ingredients:

1 cup cake flour

1 cup all-purpose flour

1 cup sugar

1 + 1/2 tsp. baking powder

1/2 tsp. table salt

1 stick chopped unsalted butter at room temperature

3/4 cup buttermilk

2 large eggs

1/2 tsp. salt

1 + 1/2 tsp. vanilla extract

Buttercream Frosting Ingredients:

2 sticks chopped unsalted butter at room temperature

3 cups powdered sugar

2 Tbsp. raspberry preserve

2 Tbsp. blackberry preserve

Baking Instructions: Preheat oven to 375f and line muffin cups. Beat butter and sugar until light and fluffy and beat in eggs one at a time. Mix all dry ingredients in fairly large mixing bowl. Add dry ingredients alternating with buttermilk. Add vanilla at the end. Divide evenly among pans and bake for 18-24 minutes and let cool in pans.

Buttercream Instructions:

Beat the butter for few minutes and start adding sugar until light and fluffy and mix in raspberry and blackberry preserve until incorporated. Frost the cupcakes and decorate with sprinkles.

Butter Cream Roses

Yields 24 cupcakes

Vanilla Cupcakes Ingredients:

1 cup cake flour

1 cup all-purpose flour

1 cup sugar

1 + 1/2 tsp. baking powder

1/2 tsp. table salt

1 stick chopped unsalted butter at room temperature

3/4 cup buttermilk

2 large eggs

1/2 tsp. salt

1 + 1/2 tsp. vanilla extract

3 Tbsp. Orange Zest

Buttercream Frosting Ingredients:

2 sticks chopped unsalted butter at room temperature

3 cups powdered sugar

1 tsp. vanilla extract

Baking Instructions: Preheat oven to 375f and line muffin cups. Beat butter and sugar until light and fluffy and beat in eggs one at a time. Mix all dry ingredients in fairly large mixing bowl. Add dry ingredients alternating with buttermilk. Add vanilla at the end. Divide evenly among pans and bake for 18-24 minutes and let cool in pans.

Buttercream Instructions:

Beat the butter for few minutes and start adding sugar until light and fluffy and mix in vanilla until incorporated. Make roses starting from inside (I learned this by watching youtube videos).

Chocolate & Cream Cheese Cupcakes

Yields 24 cupcakes

Chocolate Cupcakes Ingredients:

1 cup cake flour

1 cup all-purpose flour

1 cup sugar

1/2 cup melted dark chocolate

3/4 cup cocoa powder, unsweetened

1 + 1/2 tsp. baking powder

1/2 tsp. table salt

1 stick chopped unsalted butter at room temperature

3/4 cup milk

2 large eggs

1/2 tsp. salt

1 + 1/2 tsp. vanilla extract

Buttercream Frosting Ingredients:

2 sticks chopped unsalted butter at room temperature

3 cups powdered sugar

1 cup cream cheese at room temperature

1 tsp. vanilla extract

Baking Instructions: Preheat oven to 375f and line muffin cups. Beat butter and sugar until light and fluffy and beat in eggs one at a time. Mix all dry ingredients in fairly large mixing bowl. Add dry ingredients alternating with milk. Add vanilla at the end. Divide evenly among pans and bake for 18-24 minutes and let cool in pans.

Buttercream Instructions:

Beat the butter and cream cheese for few minutes and start adding sugar until light and fluffy and mix in vanilla until incorporated. Frost the cupcakes and decorate with sprinkles.

Hazelnuts & Caramel Cupcakes

Yields 24 cupcakes

Chocolate Cupcakes Ingredients:

1 cup cake flour

1 cup all-purpose flour

1 cup dark brown sugar

1 + 1/2 tsp. baking powder

3/4 cup cocoa powder, unsweetened

1/2 tsp. table salt

1 stick chopped unsalted butter at room temperature

3/4 cup milk

2 large eggs

1/2 tsp. salt

1 + 1/2 tsp. vanilla extract

1 cup ground hazelnuts

Caramel Frosting Ingredients:

2 sticks chopped unsalted butter at room temperature

1 cup dark brown sugar

3 cups powdered sugar

1 tsp. vanilla extract

Baking Instructions: Preheat oven to 375f and line muffin cups. Beat butter and sugar until light and fluffy and beat in eggs one at a time. Mix all dry ingredients in fairly large mixing bowl. Add dry ingredients alternating with milk. Add vanilla at the end. Divide evenly among pans and bake for 18-24 minutes and let cool in pans.

Caramel Cream Instructions:

Heat the butter and brown sugar and stir until sugar dissolves, let it cook for 2 minutes and let it cool. Once cooled, start adding powdered sugar until light and fluffy and mix in vanilla until incorporated. Frost the cupcakes and decorate with chocolate sprinkles.

Chocolate & Coconut Cupcakes

Yields 24 cupcakes

Chocolate Cupcakes Ingredients:

1 cup cake flour

1 cup all-purpose flour

1 cup sugar

3/4 cup cocoa powder, unsweetened

1 + 1/2 tsp. baking powder

1/2 tsp. table salt

3/4 cup coconut oil

3/4 cup coconut milk (or plain milk)

2 large eggs

1/2 tsp. salt

1 + 1/2 tsp. vanilla extract

1/4 cup shredded coconut

Buttercream Frosting Ingredients:

1 stick chopped unsalted butter at room temperature

1/2 cup coconut cream

1/4 cup shredded coconut

3 cups powdered sugar

1 tsp. vanilla extract

Baking Instructions: Preheat oven to 375f and line muffin cups. Beat butter and sugar until light and fluffy and beat in eggs one at a time. Mix all dry ingredients in fairly large mixing bowl. Add dry ingredients alternating with milk. Add vanilla and coconut at the end. Divide evenly among pans and bake for 18-24 minutes and let cool in pans.

Buttercream Instructions:

Beat the butter and coconut cream for few minutes and start adding sugar until light and fluffy and mix in vanilla and shredded coconut until incorporated. Frost the cupcakes and decorate with melted chocolate drizzles.

Black Forest Cupcakes

Yields 24 cupcakes

Chocolate Cupcakes Ingredients:

1 cup cake flour

1 cup all-purpose flour

1 cup sugar

1/2 cup melted dark chocolate

3/4 cup cocoa powder, unsweetened

1 + 1/2 tsp. baking powder

1/2 tsp. table salt

1 stick chopped unsalted butter at room temperature

3/4 cup buttermilk

2 large eggs

1/2 tsp. salt

1 + 1/2 tsp. vanilla extract

2 Tbsp. chopped dry cherries

Buttercream Frosting Ingredients:

2 sticks chopped unsalted butter at room temperature

3 cups powdered sugar

1 tsp. vanilla extract

Baking Instructions: Preheat oven to 375f and line muffin cups. Beat butter and sugar until light and fluffy and beat in eggs one at a time. Mix all dry ingredients in fairly large mixing bowl. Add dry ingredients alternating with buttermilk. Add vanilla at the end. Divide evenly among pans and bake for 18-24 minutes and let cool in pans.

Buttercream Instructions:

Beat the butter for few minutes and start adding sugar until light and fluffy and mix in vanilla until incorporated. Top with chocolate shavings and cherries.

Chocolate & Cream & Raspberries Cupcakes

Yields 24 cupcakes

Chocolate Cupcakes Ingredients:

1 cup cake flour

1 cup all-purpose flour

1 cup sugar

1/2 cup melted dark chocolate

3/4 cup cocoa powder, unsweetened

1 + 1/2 tsp. baking powder

1/2 tsp. table salt

1 stick chopped unsalted butter at room temperature

3/4 cup buttermilk

2 large eggs

1/2 tsp. salt

1 + 1/2 tsp. vanilla extract

Buttercream Frosting Ingredients:

2 sticks chopped unsalted butter at room temperature

3 cups powdered sugar

1 tsp. vanilla extract

Baking Instructions: Preheat oven to 375f and line muffin cups. Beat butter and sugar until light and fluffy and beat in eggs one at a time. Mix all dry ingredients in fairly large mixing bowl. Add dry ingredients alternating with buttermilk. Add vanilla at the end. Divide evenly among pans and bake for 18-24 minutes and let cool in pans.

Buttercream Instructions:
Beat the butter for few minutes and start adding sugar until light and fluffy and mix in vanilla until incorporated. Top each buttercup with 2 raspberries

Vanilla & Cream & Strawberry Cupcakes

Yields 24 cupcakes

Vanilla Cupcakes Ingredients:

1 cup cake flour

1 cup all-purpose flour

1 cup sugar

1 + 1/2 tsp. baking powder

1/2 tsp. table salt

1 stick chopped unsalted butter at room temperature

3/4 cup milk

2 large eggs

1/2 tsp. salt

1 + 1/2 tsp. vanilla extract

Buttercream Frosting Ingredients:

2 sticks chopped unsalted butter at room temperature

3 cups powdered sugar

1 tsp. vanilla extract

1/4 cup strawberry preserve

Baking Instructions: Preheat oven to 375f and line muffin cups. Beat butter and sugar until light and fluffy and beat in eggs one at a time. Mix all dry ingredients in fairly large mixing bowl. Add dry ingredients alternating with milk. Add vanilla at the end. Divide evenly among pans and bake for 18-24 minutes and let cool in pans.

Buttercream Instructions:

Beat the butter for few minutes and start adding sugar until light and fluffy and mix in vanilla and strawberry preserve until incorporated. Top with sliced strawberries.

Vanilla & Blackberry Cream Cupcakes

Yields 24 cupcakes

Vanilla Cupcakes Ingredients:

1 cup cake flour

1 cup all-purpose flour

1 cup sugar

1 + 1/2 tsp. baking powder

1/2 tsp. table salt

1 stick chopped unsalted butter at room temperature

3/4 cup Greek Yogurt

2 large eggs

1/2 tsp. salt

1 + 1/2 tsp. vanilla extract

3 Tbsp. Orange Zest

Buttercream Frosting Ingredients:

2 sticks chopped unsalted butter at room temperature

3 cups powdered sugar

1 tsp. vanilla extract

1/4 cup blackberry preserve

Baking Instructions: Preheat oven to 375f and line muffin cups. Beat butter and sugar until light and fluffy and beat in eggs one at a time. Mix all dry ingredients in fairly large mixing bowl. Add dry ingredients alternating with yogurt. Add vanilla at the end. Divide evenly among pans and bake for 18-24 minutes and let cool in pans.

Buttercream Instructions:
Beat the butter for few minutes and start adding sugar until light and fluffy and mix in vanilla and blackberry preserve until incorporated. Frost the cupcakes and decorate with sugar drizzles and sprinkles.

Chocolate & Cinnamon Anise Cream Cupcakes

Yields 24 cupcakes

Vanilla Cupcakes Ingredients:

1 cup cake flour

1 cup all-purpose flour

1 cup sugar

1 + 1/2 tsp. baking powder

1/2 tsp. table salt

1 stick chopped unsalted butter at room temperature

3/4 cup buttermilk

2 large eggs

1/2 tsp. salt

1 + 1/2 tsp. vanilla extract

3 tsp. Cinnamon

1 tsp. ground anise

Buttercream Frosting Ingredients:

2 sticks chopped unsalted butter at room temperature

3 cups powdered sugar

1 tsp. vanilla extract

3 tsp. cinnamon

Baking Instructions: Preheat oven to 375f and line muffin cups. Beat butter and sugar until light and fluffy and beat in eggs one at a time. Mix all dry ingredients in fairly large mixing bowl. Add dry ingredients alternating with buttermilk. Add vanilla at the end. Divide evenly among pans and bake for 18-24 minutes and let cool in pans.

Buttercream Instructions:

Beat the butter for few minutes and start adding sugar until light and fluffy and mix in vanilla and cinnamon until incorporated. Frost the cupcakes and decorate with sprinkles.

Vanilla And Strawberry Cream Cupcakes

Yields 24 cupcakes

Vanilla Cupcakes Ingredients:

1 cup cake flour

1 cup all-purpose flour

1 cup sugar

1 + 1/2 tsp. baking powder

1/2 tsp. table salt

1 stick chopped unsalted butter at room temperature

3/4 cup buttermilk

2 large eggs

1/2 tsp. salt

1 + 1/2 tsp. vanilla extract

2 Tbsp. ground almonds

Buttercream Frosting Ingredients:

2 sticks chopped unsalted butter at room temperature

3 cups powdered sugar

1 tsp. vanilla extract

1/4 cup strawberry preserve

Baking Instructions: Preheat oven to 375f and line muffin cups. Beat butter and sugar until light and fluffy and beat in eggs one at a time. Mix all dry ingredients in fairly large mixing bowl. Add dry ingredients alternating with buttermilk. Add vanilla and almonds at the end. Divide evenly among pans and bake for 18-24 minutes and let cool in pans.

Buttercream Instructions:

Beat the butter for few minutes and start adding sugar until light and fluffy and mix in vanilla and strawberry preserve until incorporated. Frost the cupcakes and decorate with fondant flowers.

Chocolate & Caramel Cream Cupcakes

Yields 24 cupcakes

Chocolate Cupcakes Ingredients:

1 cup cake flour

1 cup all-purpose flour

1 cup sugar

3/4 cup cocoa powder, unsweetened

1 + 1/2 tsp. baking powder

1/2 tsp. table salt

1 stick chopped unsalted butter at room temperature

3/4 cup milk

2 large eggs

1/2 tsp. salt

1 + 1/2 tsp. vanilla extract

Caramel Frosting Ingredients:

2 sticks chopped unsalted butter at room temperature

1 cup dark brown sugar

3 cups powdered sugar

1 tsp. vanilla extract

Baking Instructions: Preheat oven to 375f and line muffin cups. Beat butter and sugar until light and fluffy and beat in eggs one at a time. Mix all dry ingredients in fairly large mixing bowl. Add dry ingredients alternating with milk. Add vanilla at the end. Divide evenly among pans and bake for 18-24 minutes and let cool in pans.

Caramel Cream Instructions:
Heat the butter and brown sugar and stir until sugar dissolves, let it cook for 2 minutes and let it cool. Once cooled, start adding powdered sugar until light and fluffy and mix in vanilla until incorporated. Frost the cupcakes and decorate with fondant bunnies.

Pumpkin Cream Cupcakes

Yields 24 cupcakes

Pumpkin Cupcakes Ingredients:

1 cup cake flour

1 cup all-purpose flour

1 cup dark brown sugar

1 + 1/2 tsp. baking powder

1/2 tsp. table salt

1 stick chopped unsalted butter at room temperature

1 cup canned pumpkin puree

2 large eggs

1/2 tsp. salt

1/2 tsp. cinnamon

Pinch of nutmeg, ground

Pinch of cloves, ground

Buttercream Frosting Ingredients:

1.5 sticks chopped unsalted butter at room temperature

1/2 cup canned pumpkin puree

3 cups powdered sugar

1 tsp. vanilla extract

1/2 tsp. cinnamon

Pinch of nutmeg, ground

Baking Instructions: Preheat oven to 375f and line muffin cups. Beat butter and sugar until light and fluffy and beat in eggs one at a time. Mix all dry ingredients in fairly large mixing bowl. Add dry ingredients alternating with pumpkin puree. Add vanilla at the end. Divide evenly among pans and bake for 18-24 minutes and let cool in pans.

Buttercream Instructions:

Beat the butter for few minutes, mix in pumpkin puree and start adding sugar until light and fluffy and mix in vanilla, pumpkin puree and spices until incorporated. Frost the cupcakes and decorate with fondant flowers.

Raspberry Jam & Cream Cupcakes

Yields 24 cupcakes

Vanilla Cupcakes Ingredients:

1 cup cake flour

1 cup all-purpose flour

1 cup sugar

1 + 1/2 tsp. baking powder

1/2 tsp. table salt

1 stick chopped unsalted butter at room temperature

3/4 cup milk

2 large eggs

1/2 tsp. salt

1 + 1/2 tsp. vanilla extract

1/2 cup raspberry preserve

2 drops or 1 tsp. "no taste" red dye (depending of the type)

Buttercream Frosting Ingredients:

2 sticks chopped unsalted butter at room temperature

3 cups powdered sugar

1 tsp. vanilla extract

Baking Instructions: Preheat oven to 375f and line muffin cups. Beat butter and sugar until light and fluffy and beat in eggs one at a time. Mix all dry ingredients in fairly large mixing bowl. Add dry ingredients alternating with milk. Add vanilla and raspberry preserve at the end. Divide evenly among pans and bake for 18-24 minutes and let cool in pans.

Buttercream Instructions:

Beat the butter for few minutes and start adding sugar until light and fluffy and mix in vanilla until incorporated. Frost the cupcakes and decorate with sprinkles.

Vanilla & Banana Cream

Yields 24 cupcakes

Vanilla Cupcakes Ingredients:

1 cup cake flour

1 cup all-purpose flour

1 cup sugar

1 + 1/2 tsp. baking powder

1/2 tsp. table salt

1 stick chopped unsalted butter at room temperature

3/4 cup milk

2 large eggs

1/2 tsp. salt

1 + 1/2 tsp. vanilla extract

Buttercream Frosting Ingredients:

2 sticks chopped unsalted butter at room temperature

3 cups powdered sugar

1 tsp. vanilla extract

2 mashed ripe bananas

Baking Instructions: Preheat oven to 375f and line muffin cups. Beat butter and sugar until light and fluffy and beat in eggs one at a time. Mix all dry ingredients in fairly large mixing bowl. Add dry ingredients alternating with milk. Add vanilla at the end. Divide evenly among pans and bake for 18-24 minutes and let cool in pans.

Buttercream Instructions:
Beat the butter for few minutes and start adding sugar until light and fluffy and mix in vanilla and mashed banana until incorporated. Frost the cupcakes and decorate with sprinkles.

Oreo Cupcakes

Yields 24 cupcakes

Vanilla Cupcakes Ingredients:

1 cup cake flour

1 cup all-purpose flour

1 cup sugar

1 + 1/2 tsp. baking powder

1/2 tsp. table salt

1 stick chopped unsalted butter at room temperature

3/4 cup buttermilk

2 large eggs

1/2 tsp. salt

1 + 1/2 tsp. vanilla extract

Buttercream Frosting Ingredients:

2 sticks chopped unsalted butter at room temperature

3 cups powdered sugar

1 tsp. vanilla extract

1/2 cup Oreo cookies crumbles

Baking Instructions: Preheat oven to 375f and line muffin cups. Beat butter and sugar until light and fluffy and beat in eggs one at a time. Mix all dry ingredients in fairly large mixing bowl. Add dry ingredients alternating with buttermilk. Add vanilla at the end. Divide evenly among pans and bake for 18-24 minutes and let cool in pans.

Buttercream Instructions:

Beat the butter for few minutes and start adding sugar until light and fluffy and mix in vanilla and Oreo crumbles until incorporated. Frost the cupcakes and decorate with Oreo cookies.

Vanilla & Peach Cream Cupcakes

Yields 24 cupcakes

Vanilla Cupcakes Ingredients:

1 cup cake flour

1 cup all-purpose flour

1 cup sugar

1 + 1/2 tsp. baking powder

1/2 tsp. table salt

1 stick chopped unsalted butter at room temperature

3/4 cup milk

2 large eggs

1/2 tsp. salt

1 + 1/2 tsp. vanilla extract

Buttercream Frosting Ingredients:

2 sticks chopped unsalted butter at room temperature

3 cups powdered sugar

1 tsp. vanilla extract

1/4 cup mashed ripe peach

Baking Instructions: Preheat oven to 375f and line muffin cups. Beat butter and sugar until light and fluffy and beat in eggs one at a time. Mix all dry ingredients in fairly large mixing bowl. Add dry ingredients alternating with milk. Add vanilla at the end. Divide evenly among pans and bake for 18-24 minutes and let cool in pans.

Buttercream Instructions:

Beat the butter for few minutes and start adding sugar until light and fluffy and mix in vanilla and masher peach until incorporated. Frost the cupcakes and decorate with sprinkles and fondant leaves.

Pumpkin Spice & Cream Cupcakes

Yields 24 cupcakes

Pumpkin Cupcakes Ingredients:

1 cup cake flour

1 cup all-purpose flour

1 cup dark brown sugar

1 + 1/2 tsp. baking powder

1/2 tsp. table salt

1 stick chopped unsalted butter at room temperature

1 cup canned pumpkin puree

2 large eggs

1/2 tsp. salt

1/2 tsp. cinnamon

Pinch of nutmeg, ground

Pinch of cloves, ground

Buttercream Frosting Ingredients:

2 sticks chopped unsalted butter at room temperature

3 cups powdered sugar

1 tsp. cinnamon

1/4 tsp. nutmeg, ground

1/4 tsp. cloves, ground

Baking Instructions: Preheat oven to 375f and line muffin cups. Beat butter and sugar until light and fluffy and beat in eggs one at a time. Mix all dry ingredients in fairly large mixing bowl. Add dry ingredients alternating with pumpkin. Add spices at the end. Divide evenly among pans and bake for 18-24 minutes and let cool in pans.

Buttercream Instructions:

Beat the butter for few minutes and start adding sugar until light and fluffy and mix in spices until incorporated. Sprinkle with cinnamon.

Vanilla & Blackberry Cream Cupcakes

Yields 24 cupcakes

Vanilla Cupcakes Ingredients:

1 cup cake flour

1 cup all-purpose flour

1 cup sugar

1 + 1/2 tsp. baking powder

1/2 tsp. table salt

1 stick chopped unsalted butter at room temperature

3/4 cup buttermilk

2 large eggs

1/2 tsp. salt

1 + 1/2 tsp. vanilla extract

3 Tbsp. Lemon Zest

Buttercream Frosting Ingredients:

2 sticks chopped unsalted butter at room temperature

3 cups powdered sugar

1 tsp. vanilla extract

1/4 cup blackberry preserve

Baking Instructions: Preheat oven to 375f and line muffin cups. Beat butter and sugar until light and fluffy and beat in eggs one at a time. Mix all dry ingredients in fairly large mixing bowl. Add dry ingredients alternating with buttermilk. Add vanilla at the end. Divide evenly among pans and bake for 18-24 minutes and let cool in pans.

Buttercream Instructions:

Beat the butter for few minutes and start adding sugar until light and fluffy and mix in vanilla and blackberry preserve until incorporated. Frost the cupcakes and decorate with sprinkles.

www.ingramcontent.com/pod-product-compliance
Lightning Source LLC
Chambersburg PA
CBHW070917080526
44589CB00013B/1339